A BOOK
TO GIVE YOU
HOPE

Naomi Navec

Edited by Roland Gugganig

Cover picture by Evie Shaffer

Printed in the United States of America.

ISBN: 979-8-8410-2591-7

This book is dedicated to anyone in need of hope.

To all of us.

Our prime purpose in this life is to help others, and if you can't help them, at least don't hurt them.

Dalai Lama

CONTENTS

Acknowledgments

I would like to acknowledge the enormous help given to me in creating this book. For their encouragement, patience and guidance, I wish to thank my best friends Ruth Miscoria, Rita Tissieres, and Anthony Johnson.

Also, a special thanks to my makers, Jean-A-P and Marie-J-P, my sister Chad and my brother Eliezer.

My special people, Amour Salim, Lyse Bouity, Sara Poaty, Horla Ray, Anna Tk, Matthew Hollis, David Jackson, Gustavo Lopez, Drhephes Keeda, Christian Kavitah and aunty Dominique. My editor, Roland Gugganig for handling this project with just the right touch.

And as always, my appreciation to my online community who have personally requested a compilation of my quotes in a manuscript. Thank you all for your love. I hope this book blesses and inspires you even more.

RELATIONSHIPS

You are under no obligation to build a close relationship with people just because you are related by blood.

Family is the people who love you, who make you feel at home, people you can trust, people who want the best for you.

You don't choose the family you're born in, but you can choose the family you stay in.

Some relationships are like glasses. If they break in big pieces, there's still hope to put them back together

But if they break in very tiny pieces, it makes it more challenging to fix.

Sometimes you just have to accept that it's time to let go. That certain things should stay broken because they're too damaged to go back to how they used to be.

People grow apart, everything changes and life goes on.

Everyone we love is going to leave us someday. Either through death or the uncertainty of life.

So cherish every moment you have with the people you love while they're still here. It's not going to last forever.

Call people who call you, worry about people who are worried about you, check on people who check on you. Invest in relationships where the efforts are mutual.

Give up on anything low-vibrational and one sided.

You shouldn't be the only one to always try to keep people in your life. People should be afraid of losing you too.

It's time to put yourself first.

Life is a paradox, it has an amazing way of turning tables around. You can be at your lowest today, people can neglect you but tomorrow holds a different story.

One day, the tables will turn. You will gain your power back and the same people who once enjoyed seeing you struggle, will be the same ones to envy your success and happiness.

If people have mistreated you, don't stay where they left you. Choose to level up. Succeed, and you will be shedding tears of joy in the end.

If there's something you don't want people to talk about, then don't tell anyone about it. People can only gossip about something that's already out there.

The moment you decide to tell someone your business, just know there are chances they will also go tell someone else about it.

So unless you really don't care that it gets out there, then try to be more private with your life.

Noisy people are everywhere. People who like to gossip about everyone, will also gossip about you to others.

Don't post everything you feel. Don't say everything you think. Don't tell people things you wouldn't be comfortable having everyone know about. Unless they're really really trustworthy.

Being an open book comes with a price tag. **The world doesn't need to know you like that.** Have some privacy. Move in silence.

Be careful who you hurt in this life.
Some tears carry curses.

If you want to live a full life and be completely free, **stop caring about what people think about you.**

It can be challenging because nobody likes the idea of being disliked, criticized or judged but if you can get to a place in life where you decide to no longer let what people think, say and how they feel about you affect you, you will unlock an awesome level of freedom.

Most people say they don't care, but usually those who try their best to prove that they don't care, usually care the most. If you truly want to stop caring, don't feel the need to explain yourself to anyone. Just don't care.

The happiest people are free. They're free because they don't let others dictate their lives. They don't have an image to maintain. They are not people pleasers.

So do what makes you happy regardless of what it looks like to others. As long as you're not harming anyone, you're good to go.

People will still criticize you especially when they don't agree with your choices and can't control you; but with time, they will leave you alone when they realize that nothing they do or say affects you in any way.

You will meet all types of people in this life:

People who will hurt you, who will misunderstand you, who won't see the real you, who will use you…

But you will also meet people who will see through you, embrace your flaws and brokenness, and despite everything, they will choose to stick around and love you just the way you are.

I truly hope that life will someday reward you with unconditional love from genuine people.

It will heal you.

If you feel like you don't fit into society's standards of beauty, just remind yourself that nobody is perfect and that you're enough just the way you are.

Beauty is in the eye of the beholder and it goes beyond the physical.

Improve your appearance if you want to, but only do it for yourself; not to conform into anyones standards.

Also remember that there's a type for everyone. You don't have to look a certain way for someone to love you.

Love doesn't cost a thing. The heart wants what it wants and it has reasons that the mind will never understand.

They are not thinking about you, not missing you, not worried about you and not sorry.

I know it's hard but stay strong.

Attachment is the root of suffering. The moment you detach from someone you think you can't live without, they'll become ordinary in your eyes and you won't even care that they're no longer in your life.

In a couple years from today, after you grieve and heal, you won't even remember or think about them.

But they will remember you, and how loved you made them feel. It will hit them really hard to realize they lost someone who loved them especially if they fail to replace you.

Try your best to live in as much peace and harmony with people in your life. Don't just spread love, be love.

You don't have to befriend everyone but at least have some good connections.

Avoid unnecessary drama, conflicts and situations that disturb your peace.

To struggle with peace is too expensive.

Everyone you meet in life is a teacher who comes to serve their purpose on your journey.

Realizing this will make the healing, forgiving, and detachment process a little lighter when their time to leave your life will come.

It will still hurt, but having the understanding that everything they did was necessary for your growth and development, will make it easier to process.

Thank them for the lessons because without them you wouldn't have gained all the wisdom, maturity, and strength you now have.

Have you ever been ghosted?

Everything was going so well between you and someone, then all of a sudden they cut off all communication.

People ghost for different reasons but fear is one of the main reasons. Fear of commitment, fear of intimacy, fear of honesty…

So how do you handle being ghosted?

1- Reach out to try to seek closure. You kindly ask them what went wrong and maybe they'll tell you the truth.

2- You mirror them back by going no contact. You remind yourself that ghosting you has nothing to do with your value.

Don't ever chase a ghost. The responsibility to fix the connection should 100% be on them. You deserve a lot better than that.

Put some respect on your name and take your power back by moving on peacefully with your life.

People won't always be happy for you, but that doesn't mean you should stop living your life.

You're not responsible for people's happiness. You're responsible for your own.

If people aren't happy in their lives and can't stand the fact that you're happy in yours, then that's their problem, not yours.

Don't dim your light just because you fear people will hate and be jealous of you.

Be happy, you owe yourself that.

Don't let people cross your boundaries by thinking that it's the only way you can create peace with them.

When a person isn't meant for you, they will take away your peace and bring in a lot of confusion and pain in your life.

You will give your all, but it will never be enough. They won't see your light no matter how great of a person you are.

You are the only person you can't live without. You will be fine without them.

Please be kind to everybody you meet, you never know what someone is going through behind the curtain

Hurting someone's feelings is like throwing a rock in the ocean, but do you know how deep that rock can go?

Everyone you meet is battling something they're not openly expressive about.

People are hurting in silence.

All it takes is one negative word to trigger someone and break them apart forever.

Please, be kind.

Rejection has a lot more to do with the person rejecting than the person rejected. Understanding this will save you from a lot of suffering.

When people get rejected, they tend to think that it's because they're not good enough or that there's something wrong with them.

But you must understand that rejection has nothing to do with you. They are rejecting you because of themselves. Try not to take it personally, there's nothing wrong with you.

Think of yourself as an apple and the person who rejected you prefers oranges.

Does the fact that they don't like apples mean there's something wrong with apples? Of course not.

Don't worry about who doesn't prefer you, just know that there are so many people in the world who love apples. **One's trash is another's treasure, one's pain is another's pleasure.**

People will push and press you until you snap back. Then they'll say you're overly sensitive and turn themselves into your victim.

They will disappoint you over and over and then ask you why you have trust issues.

They will bring out the worst in you by stabbing you in the back then asking you why you're bleeding.

People will hurt you and act like you hurt them.

But before you react, remember this:

People who have a low self-esteem are always bringing others down. People who are miserable are always hurting others. People who are insecure will always try to make you feel like you're below them.

Because people's actions are a reflection of how they feel about themselves. It's called projection!

People who are angry and mean to you are hurt.

They are making you suffer because deep within themselves, they are also suffering.

Underneath that anger, there are layers of pain and sadness.

It's hard to not take it personally but remind yourself that their actions have nothing to do with you. They are dealing with old wounds.

That doesn't excuse their behaviour, but looking at it from this perspective will help you depersonalize the hurt they projected on you.

They don't need punishment, they need healing, love and help.

Shoutout to all the misfits, the outcasts, the rule breakers, the weirdos, the loners, the outsiders, the rebels that exist within our society.

Thank you for growing into your strangeness and making it a workable identity. Being the odd one can make it hard to fit in, but that's the beauty of it.

If we didn't have people like you in this society, the world would be so bland. So don't ever let anyone make you feel like there's something wrong with you just because you're different.

We are supposed to be different.

Diversity makes the beauty of this planet.

Would you rather live in a world where everyone was identical?

Before you decide to give up, think about all the people who would want to see you fail. Just pause and think.

How does the idea of knowing that some people would be happy to see you unhappy, broken and miserable makes you feel?

This is strangely motivating but let your haters be your motivation to keep going. Outlive them!

Giving up on yourself would be like letting them win.

The saying "trust nobody" doesn't literally mean to not trust anyone.

You can trust people who have earned your trust, but you must know that there are different levels of trust. And that no matter how much you trust someone, you should still keep a good percentage of some trust to yourself because people are unpredictable.

You can trust people, but you should never put 100% trust in a human.

And when you fall apart with someone, keep the secrets they shared with you, to yourself. Don't backstab them.

Who you surround yourself with has a strong impact on your peace.

So surround yourself with people who energize you, not those who drain you.

If someone is not bringing peace to your life, then they don't need to be in your life.

It's better to be alone than to be around the wrong people. **It's better to struggle with loneliness than with peace.**

Don't regret all the good you've done to people who chose to be ungrateful in return.

If what you did came from a place of kindness and love, then you did something beautiful.

Don't let people's ungratefulness discourage you from continuing doing good in life.

Doing good to someone doesn't mean they should do the same for you in return. That's not what gratitude is about.

To be grateful means to show appreciation.

Some people don't show appreciation. You help them and the moment you no longer can, they act like you're a bad person and forget all the good you once did.

Their appreciation for you is only conditioned on how much they can gain from you.

The right people to have in your life, will inspire and encourage you to accomplish great things. They will be a solid shoulder to lean on in times of turmoil.

They will help you become a better person and make you feel loved and appreciated.

The right people will be a blessing to your life.

When you look into your life, can you at least name one person who fits into this description?

What kind of people are you surrounded by?

Just think about this.

Do you realize how rare it has become in today's society to find trustworthy people with genuine intentions, values, and morals?

When you find someone real who loves and cares for you, don't look for someone "better" because what you think might be better could just be an illusion.

When you're in a boxing ring, and your opponents know your weaknesses, they're going to keep hitting you on your sensitive spots in order to defeat you.

People who know how to hurt you, will constantly keep triggering you to get a reaction out of you.

That's why it's important to grow stronger around your fears and insecurities and to not allow yourself to be vulnerable with everyone.

Don't give anyone the power to bring back the triggered version of you that you worked so hard to heal.

People will leave your life then try to come back and expect you to be exactly where they left you and for things to get back to how they used to be.

Just like that.

Don't let anyone think that they can walk in and out of your life whenever it's convenient. **You are nobody's doormat.**

If you want to let someone back in, don't make it easy for them. **Hold them accountable for their actions** and have them work on earning your trust again.

You disrespect yourself every time you chase after people who have shown you several times that they don't care or respect you.

You disrespect yourself when you don't speak up when people cross your boundaries; when you're too nice all the time.

Systematically withdraw from anyone who doesn't give you back the same energy you give out. You don't have to be loyal to people who take you for granted.

How people treat you is more important than how much you like them.

Never think that someone is too good for you. Never make yourself feel like you're not good enough for someone. It's all in your head.

Nobody is too good for you and no matter how imperfect or broken we are, **we all deserve love.**

Don't put people on a pedestal. Nobody is perfect!

Be confident in your skin and let go of your fears of abandonment and rejection.

Love people, but don't worship them or think you're below them.

The wrong people will find you in peace and leave you in pieces. The right people will find you in pieces and lead you to peace.

Unknown author

Put some order in your life by focusing on yourself.

Start living your best life, do things that make you happy and give you peace. Take good care of your physical, mental and emotional health.

Stop paying attention to people who don't care about you and who are negative. Surround yourself with the right people.

Create a meaningful life that gives you peace.

Being too nice all the time won't get anyone to respect or value you. It will get people to use you.

Nice people are targets to being taken advantage of because they don't usually have boundaries. They over-give and overdo.

People will take advantage of you and breadcrumb you when you have no boundaries.

Boundaries will earn you respect. Nobody is going to mess around with someone who stands up for themselves.

You can have a big heart and still learn to say no. Don't let people use you!

A lot of people won't believe in you.

They will make you feel like you're not good enough, that you're a failure, that you're hard to love…

Stay away from people like that.

Their negativity can only affect you if you decide to believe them.

It's about time you unlearn all the toxic things you've learned from people who were at war with themselves.

Your feelings matter
Your pain matters
Your dreams matter
Your story matters
Your voice matters
Your life matters

You matter!

Sometimes the problem isn't them, it's you.

You say you want loyalty, love and respect but you keep entertaining and chasing after people who are giving you the opposite.

Why are you doing this to yourself?

You have to know what you want. Quit wasting time on people who aren't good for you. Find the strength to emotionally detach from people who are walking in the opposite direction of where you want to be.

Realize that they're only doing what they're doing because you're allowing them to.

You hold the power!

Nobody is a saint, nobody is perfect. People who act like they are, are lying to themselves.

Being religious doesn't make anyone a good person. Being non-religious doesn't make anyone a bad person.

We are not defined by our beliefs or lack of beliefs. We are defined by the way we live, love and treat each other.

You will recognize God in a person by their fruits. And it's more than just a label, it's a lifestyle.

If you miss someone, tell them. You want to see them? Plan it. There's been a misunderstanding? Explain your point of view.

Do you have doubts? ask for clarity. You don't like something they did? Let them know.

People aren't in your head to know what you're thinking. Express your heart. Living in fear, ego and pride is a waste of life. **We won't be here forever to be living like we got time.**

People who feel the need to bring others down in order to feel powerful are the weakest.

They may act all strong on the outside but deep inside, they are unsecured.

That's why they need to put on a facade to protect themselves from getting hurt. It's their ego.

The best way to win with people who are unkind, is to refuse to play. Don't react or engage in their negativity.

Before you argue or engage in a conversation with someone, ask yourself if they're open-minded enough to even grasp **the concept of different perspectives.**

Because if they're not, there's no point in trying to explain yourself to them. You will waste your time and energy going back and forth trying to make them understand your point.

Sometimes, keeping your thoughts and opinions to yourself is the best way to protect your peace. Accept that some people won't ever change their mind, no matter what you tell them.

One thing you should know about extremely kind and loving people is that their other side can be just as extreme.

Two people can go through the same hell, one will come out bitter while the other will be more compassionate because they'd have an understanding of what being hurt feels like.

Don't mistake their self-control and loving nature for weakness. **The beast in them is asleep, not dead.**

There's a difference between fighting for someone who loves you and fighting someone to love you.

A point will come where you're going to have to ask yourself if you're being patient or just wasting your time.

If it feels forced, please stop. If it's one sided, please stop. If it makes you feel worthless, please stop. If it requires you to be someone you're not, please stop!

Only be where you feel wanted, safe and respected.

Stay away from everything that makes you feel less.

Be so completely yourself, that everyone else can feel encouraged to be themselves around you.

Be so loving, kind and nonjudgmental that people can feel safe around your energy.

Safe enough to also be themselves, to speak their truth, to express their feelings with no fear.

To feel safe and at peace around someone's energy is a different level of intimacy and love.

Home is where you're loved and comfortable enough to be yourself.

Home is also where your feelings are taken into consideration; where you are accepted, where you can speak and live your truth.

Home is not just a place, home is a feeling.

Actions don't always speak louder than words. Don't just believe words or actions cause people can fake emotions too and put on an act to make you believe a false reality.

Someone can care about you and act like they don't. People say they don't care, but do they really not?

Someone can tell you the opposite of what they feel. Many people are good at pretending.

Trust patterns, trust energies, and your intuition.

Actions can unfortunately be deceptive too.

Some people are good at manipulating others by putting on a facade with their actions just to get something from them.

The good news is that people can't pretend forever. A day will come where the truth will be known.

If you have no good intentions towards someone, **please leave them alone.**

Don't walk into their lives deciding to add more pain.

The hurt you may cause can have a long term impact on them.

Way too many people are already really sad and heartbroken.

The last thing they need is more hurt.

Make your life simple by **focusing on people who love and care about you**, not on people who don't.

Why choose to let those who take you for granted be the center of your life when you have so many people who actually care?

You know what I'm saying?

Love the heart that hurts you, but never hurt the heart that loves you.

Vipin Sharma

No message is a message.

Respect people's boundaries and need for space. People can't be social everyday. When a person goes MIA (missing in action), they're giving you a message.

It could mean anything from: I am not feeling my best, I have no energy to be social, I am feeling sad, overwhelmed; I'm going through a lot and I need space to deal with my emotions...

Try not to overthink their silence unless you're worried about their safety.

When they're ready to talk to you again, they will come back on their own. And if they don't ever, well, life will go on.

Avoid conversations that involve hating other people.

It's so easy to get carried away with gossip because it can be entertaining, but remember that you don't have to engage in hate.

Stay away from people who are always talking about others. Befriend people you can **learn something constructive from.**

Trying to build a healthy relationship with a person who's mentally unstable is like trying to drive a car that has no break. You will end up crashing in a mental health institution.

You cannot fix a problem a person has with themselves, you are not their therapist. They have to do the work.

You can help along the way, but they need to be the ones desperate for a change.

In times of conflict always remember this:

It's not you against them, it's you and them against the problem.

For example, if someone lied to you, the problem is not them, the problem is the lie they told.

When you learn to separate the source of the problem from the person, it will make it easier to resolve.

If you want to have a heart-to-heart conversation with someone, call them or talk to them face to face.

Avoid sending a text, unless that's the only option you have. A lot can be misunderstood through text. Especially the tone of your message.

Real conversations should be done face to face with good eye contact.

The real monsters are humans.

When you don't release your emotions, it creates an attachment to the situation and the people involved.

The more you hold onto these emotions, the more you will hurt and the longer you will take to heal.

Suppressing your emotions will hold you back in the past. If you want to heal, you have to feel and release these emotions.

A young mind thinks:

I can't live without this person

A mature mind says:

People come and go, they're not the last human left on earth. Their time in my life is done. As much as it hurts, **I have to detach because life has to go on.**

Avoid stalking the people you're trying to heal from.

Feeding off their lives will not help you move on. You have to focus on yourself and resist the urge to look back at what they're up to.

You have to resist until you get to the point where you no longer care.

You will break your own heart by checking on the past.

People post their happiest versions online, don't feed off their lives.

Focus on yourself.

Don't let people's failures influence your journey.

Our paths have been traced differently.

Just because they walked down the same path and didn't succeed doesn't mean it will also be the same for you.

You're not them.

Have the courage to test the waters for yourself. You never know what doors you can unlock.

Be careful who you allow back in your life when you're feeling weak. Some people will only come back to test you; to see if they still have access, power and control over you.

Why they come back:

1- They genuinely missed you, realized your worth and want to reconcile.

2- They see you're doing good without them; they want to distract you.

3- They realized they were wrong, they're genuinely sorry.

4- They failed to replace you.

5- They want you now that they can't have you.

6- Their other options didn't work out.

7- They're feeling lonely and want you to boost their ego.

8- They've done some work on themselves, they're ready to be with you now.

Whatever their reason is, be on your guards.

You can do so many things right but some people will only talk about your mistakes and flaws to judge and define you.

Moral of the story:

Do what's right but don't spend too much time trying to prove yourself to people.

Don't be a people pleaser.

If someone wants to leave your life, let them leave.

Don't hold anyone back, especially if you know you did your best to keep them around.

Let people do what they want to do so you know what they'd rather do.

Let them go find their happiness.

There will always be people who won't appreciate you in this life. **Don't lose yourself trying to keep them in your life**, it's not worth the sacrifice.

If people can't appreciate the love you bring to the table, take your love and give it to those who will.

Don't let your feelings and emotions overpower your intelligence and self-respect.

Nothing is guaranteed in life. People change, seasons end, life happens.

But just because nothing is guaranteed doesn't mean you shouldn't take risks.

What if you try and it actually works out this time? what if? ...

If all you do is let your fears control your life, you will end up missing out on your blessings.

Get busy with your own life. Occupy your mind with your priorities. Disconnect from people and the things that are distracting or hindering you from making progress.

People who are busy don't have time to gossip or compare their lives to others. Busy people are focused on their goals.

Surround yourself with inspiring people. Make no room for negativity in your circle. Mind your own business too.

We live in a world where people are afraid of being themselves because they don't wanna be judged by other people who are also afraid of being themselves.

lol

Learn from other people's mistakes.

Something doesn't have to personally happen to you for it to be a lesson. Watch people and learn from their mistakes.

Everyone you meet in life has something new to teach you even when what happens to them doesn't directly involve you.

The person who is the least interested and invested in a relationship, controls the relationship.

If you feel your relationship with someone is falling out of balance, the best thing you can do is pull back- Stop giving too much affection.

It's very unfortunate that we live in times where showing too much heart makes people take you for granted.

If they can't appreciate your presence, give them a taste of your absence.

Some people will only start caring about you when you stop caring about them and will only notice you're there when you're no longer there.

Don't expect support from familiar faces.

People in your entourage could be the last ones to support you because of their jealousy or lack of interest.

Don't take it personally and don't let it discourage you.

Remember why you started in the first place and keep doing what you love regardless of who supports you or doesn't.

All men aren't the same. All women aren't the same.

All (insert stereotype) aren't the same. It's the people you've dealt with that were the same.

People need to be judged as individuals, not groups.

Don't blame an entire group of people based on what a couple of them have done.

One person doesn't represent everyone.

Don't stay where people left you. No matter what happens, you have to find your way back up.

Rise from your ashes like a phoenix.

Life goes on, level up.

Forgiveness doesn't equal reconciliation. Reconciliation is a personal choice, not an obligation.

You can forgive someone and still choose to remain distant and indifferent towards them. That doesn't make you bitter.

It's like getting bitten by a snake then recovering from that bite. Does healing mean you have to expose yourself to the snake again?

Forgiveness is not about forgetting or pretending it didn't happen. **Forgiveness is a personal choice one makes to heal and liberate themselves from the prison of bitterness.** It's about taking your power back and moving on from the past.

It's not about reconciling with those who once caused you a lot of suffering. That's up to you to decide, not others.

Nobody is perfect. We all make mistakes because we're humans. So when you fall short, don't beat yourself down. Always find your way back up by forgiving and healing yourself.

Don't waste your life living in the past. All experiences are lessons. Take what they taught you and grow into a better version of yourself.

Wishing you never met them, never made that decision, or that certain things never happened won't change the fact that they did.

Life will always test and challenge you regardless of how careful you try to be.

Some things happen in life because of our bad decisions but some others happen because they're supposed to happen. Call it fate or destiny but some paths are inevitable.

So find a way to forgive yourself for whatever happened in the past. Forgive the experience too. Grow from it and choose to become a better person.

They say that when you truly love someone, you can't ever unlove them because unloving them would mean the love was never real. That's not true!

Love is like a flower, if you water and care for it, it will bloom. If you neglect it, it will die. You water love with commitment, loyalty, communication, respect. You kill it with the opposite.

Never think that someone who loves you today will always love you, regardless of how you treat them.

Even the strongest emotion expires when ignored or taken for granted.

A couple who had been together for more than 60 years were interviewed and asked what was the secret of their healthy relationship. They said:

"We never threw away our plants when the thorns grew on them. We simply removed the thorns."

In other words, they addressed their conflicts with clarity without bottling them in.

You know, the conversations you feel uncomfortable having with people close to you are usually the ones that hold the key to clarity, peace and reconciliation.

The cure for the pain is in the pain.

When someone you love frustrates you, let them know. Communicate your feelings. Don't expect them to just guess or notice that they've offended you.

If you don't fix the little problems, they'll turn into bigger issues and that will lead to the collapse of the entire relationship.

This applies to all types of relationships, not just romantic ones.

Abuse is not always physical. Abuse is also control, disrespect, and hurtful words.

Protect yourself from people who are not kind. Try to stay away from those who are committed to their toxic ways, it's not worth the energy.

Ignore, block and distance yourself from people who don't care about your feelings.

Words are so powerful they can leave a permanent scar in your mind. So protect your peace at all costs.

When someone makes a mistake, don't suddenly forget all the good they've done; especially if they have been more good to you than bad.

People aren't defined by their flaws.

Was there ever a time where they were good to you? Can you think of a moment when they made a positive gesture that really touched your heart?

Perhaps that's where your focus should be, to remind yourself that they're not bad people after all and that they deserve a second chance.

Making fun of someone's physical appearance is the lowest thing a person can ever do.

People don't get to choose their faces, bodies or genetics. To bring someone down because of a physical feature they have no control over is super immature.

We live inside these bodies. We are not these bodies.

People who think so highly of themselves because of their looks are extremely superficial.

To think highly of oneself is not a bad thing, the problem comes when these thoughts create a complex of superiority.

To feel superior or more important than another person because of a privilege you have that they don't, is self-deception.

Because **death is our greatest equalizer.**

No matter who you are, what you look like and what you have in this life, you won't get a privilege from death for being all that.

Let's be humble, everything else is vanity.

Let's be kind, everything will stay behind.

Let's be loving, we won't be here forever!

If it's not relationship issues, it's finances. If it's not finances, it's physical/mental health. If it's not health, it's work/school drama. If it's not drama, it's something else…

There's always something going on in life.

To think that there are people who are dealing with all of the above at once is heartbreaking.

It really does take a lot of mental resilience to remain sane in such an insane world.

Sending out love, courage and strength to everyone feeling super overwhelmed and exhausted by life.

Think about someone today, and randomly send them a text to remind them of how much you appreciate and love them.

It may just be a text to you, but it could mean the world to them. People need to constantly be reminded that they're loved and appreciated.

I once read a story about a person who was feeling suicidal and they randomly got a text from someone saying:

"Hey, it's been a while, I'm thinking about you" and that text saved their lives, they realized someone cared.

Don't be the reason someone goes to bed feeling unloved or the reason they hate themselves. Try to be the light in people's lives.

Choose to be the reason someone smiles today. Make their day!

It's better to be single than to be in a toxic relationship. It's better to be single than to be in a relationship where you feel alone.

It's better to be single than to be in a relationship where you feel unappreciated, unloved or taken for granted.

To be single is not a crime. People fear being alone but do you know what's worse than loneliness?

Being with someone who makes you feel miserable.

Love is a beautiful thing when it's true, healthy and reciprocated. Having someone by your side to build a life with is a wonderful thing.

Relationships aren't perfect, but there's a difference between being in a relationship that has ups and downs and being in a toxic one.

A romantic partner is supposed to bring light in your life, not create darkness.

Breaking free from a toxic and unhealthy relationship or love situation is really hard but a time will come where you're going to have to choose between loving them and loving yourself.

I hope you choose yourself.

They are not the last human left on earth. They can be replaced!

One of my favourite spiritual principles to live by is always to try to leave everything in better condition than I found it: Apartments, hotel rooms, libraries and yes, people's lives too.

After every interaction, ask yourself:

"Did I leave this person in better condition than I found them? Did I uplift, inspire, empower them? Did I cheer them up? Did I make them laugh? Did I give some love and support?"

If you approach social interactions with this simple intention, you will always know what to do.

Be the change you want to see happen in this world.

There's so much pain in the world. So much hurt, cruelty, insensitivity, greed, hatred; So much negativity and yet so much indifference to it.

Don't wake up today choosing to add another problem in the world; choose to be good, do better.

Be someone's blessing, be kind, be loving, be real, be helpful; make a difference in someone's life.

When someone throws their hate on you, and you don't react back, that hate will stay with them.

People's negativity can only affect you if you decide to take part in it by responding.

Someone sends you a nasty message? Don't read it. They say something mean? Ignore them!

Refuse to bring yourself to their level.

Your lack of reaction will backlash on their own emotions and cause them more frustration.

Find the courage to tell people who you truly are.

Be honest about what you stand for too. Tell them!

Pretending is a heavy burden to carry. Set yourself free. That's the bravest thing you can ever do.

You can't pretend forever. You're going to have to speak your truth; at some point it's gonna get too heavy on your chest.

The only thing you're risking is rejection but remember, it's better to be rejected for being who you truly are than to be accepted for being someone you're not.

When you're destined for greatness, you will come across a lot of people who will try their best to bring you down by making you doubt yourself to set you up for failure.

But see, the secret is to have self-awareness.

When you know who you are, you won't really be moved by people's misjudgments and criticism of you.

When it's time to move on from a relationship, change career, or leave a place behind, you'll just know.

You will feel purposeless staying behind. Your life will no longer make sense. You just won't feel happy anymore.

Staying behind will feel forced and meaningless!

If you bow down to other people's standards and expectations, you will only attract people that won't see your worth.

If you keep trying to change yourself to be liked by other people, you will eventually lose yourself.

THIS IS HOW YOU KNOW SOMEONE IS JEALOUS OF YOU

1- They invalidate your accomplishments by comparing you to others to make you feel like you're not doing enough.

2- They imitate you and try to compete with you. They will always want what you have.

3- They make little hateful jokes. For example, they could say something like:

"Don't get too excited, some people are doing better than you, just kidding."

4- They ghost you when you tell them good news. They don't react with happiness. They may even fake being happy for you but you won't hear much from them after a while.

5- They use someone else to project their jealousy. For example, they could say something like:

"People are going to be so jealous of you if they find out how good you're doing." Those are their own feelings.

6- They will constantly give you bad advice to demotivate and discourage you.

7- They won't show up when you're celebrating your success. They may hardly congratulate you for anything you do great but they'll be the first ones to criticize you when you make a mistake.

8- They talk bad about you behind your back. You won't know this but with time, someone will report back all the things that have been said about you by this person. It's a small world.

9- You just feel like you can't trust them, the vibe just feels off with them. Notice, when you tell them something exciting, things go bad in your life after. That's because they are the bad eye.

10- You will find them in the same circle with those who don't like you. If anyone is close to someone who hates you, just know they have something in common.

If anyone came to your mind while reading this. Please be careful. Energy never lies. A jealous person is dangerous to have around.

Self-Love
and
Awareness

When a plane crashes, it alarms the world but people tend to forget that traveling by air is really safe.

One bad thing happens and the world focuses on it. What if we did the opposite?

You'll see people focus on the negative aspect of life, "Oh well, so many people are unhappy in relationships, so many people are sad, there's so much of x and y."

Yeah there is but there are also a lot of happy people with successful stories and relationships, why don't people talk about that?

My point is, there's more to life than negativity. Don't let the world turn you cold. Just because there's a lot of sadness and pain in the world doesn't mean your life has to flow on that vibration.

People's constant disappointments and negativity will make you lose faith in humanity, but remind yourself that you don't have to focus on the negative aspect of life. Choose to look at life from a brighter perspective.

Sometimes the problem itself is not the problem. Sometimes the problem is the way you approach and handle the problem.

Your conclusion, thoughts and beliefs about a situation can sometimes cause more pain and suffering than the actual reality of it.

Misjudging a situation can aggravate the experience. So take a step back, clear off your mind, and try to see things from a different perspective.

Change the way you look at things and the things you look at will change.

Regardless of what happens, don't change who you are. Don't become like the people who hurt you. Choose to be better.

Trust me on this one, there are people in this world who are looking for people like you.

People with good hearts, values and intentions have become so rare that so many people will treasure what you have to offer.

You have value, don't ever take yourself for granted.

Keep a journal of positive affirmation.

Write down all the wonderful things about yourself: your achievements, your qualities, your blessings...

Every time you start to doubt yourself, or when people project their negativity on you, go back to that journal and **read what you wrote.**

People who have been deeply hurt tend to build walls to protect themselves. Protecting yourself is a great thing, but how long will you stay in your comfort zone?

Nobody is meant to go through life in complete isolation. Human interactions and relationships are important. You don't have to befriend or trust people, but you should at least have some good connections. Don't shut the whole world down.

Focusing too hard on protecting your heart will help you avoid pain, but it will also make you miss out on building happy memories with good people.

Do what feels best for you, and when you're ready to go out in the world again, wear your best smile.

Living in fear of getting hurt again, won't actually stop you from getting hurt, it will only stop you from enjoying life.

Nobody has all the answers to life. Even monks, gurus, pastors, life coaches, therapists have unanswered questions. Nobody will ever completely figure life out because life is a mystery and we are all students on a journey to learn.

So when someone gives you advice/guidance, always use your discernment before making a decision.

If something doesn't resonate with your inner being, reject it. No matter who it's coming from.

Your intuition is your inner compass, listen to it.

Sometimes seeking answers can misguide, trigger and confuse you even more, especially when you're feeling hopeless and vulnerable.

So be careful who you seek guidance from.

And if you can't tune into your intuition, be okay with not having answers. **Don't drive yourself crazy trying to understand life.**

Just because someone isn't expressing regret for what they did to you, doesn't mean they're not feeling it. You don't know what's happening in their head. It could be hitting them harder than it's hitting you.

Everyone doesn't have the courage and humility to take that leap of faith to make things right with those they've hurt. People have their ways of showing regret and it's not always verbal.

Some people do let their pride and fears get in the way, but that doesn't mean they're not aware of what they have done.

But whatever their reasons are, **know that you do deserve an apology.**

And if you did move on with your life without ever receiving that apology, then you should really be proud of yourself.

The reality is, you cannot make anyone appreciate you, stay in your life, value you, make time for you or care for you.

Unless they really want to do it, you can't force them to because everyone has free will.

So **appreciate the people who chose to stay in your life voluntarily.**

When you really think deeply about life, you'll realize that resentment and selfishness are not worth your energy.

Our time in this life is limited. It's okay to be angry and to feel hurt, but spending the rest of your life being bitter is a waste of life.

Everything will stay behind someday, the most important thing is to try to live a peaceful and happy life.

In a couple of years from today, people won't really remember what brand of clothes you wore, how you looked or what car you drove...

People will remember how you treated them and how you made them feel.

People never forget how you make them feel, so try your best to be a good memory to someone.

Make your heart the most beautiful thing about you. There are beautiful faces and intelligent minds everywhere.

But a beautiful heart will always remain beautiful no matter the time that passes by.

A beautiful heart is kind, compassionate, caring, peaceful, humble, loving, true, honest, forgiving and understanding.

What are you grateful for? Can you think of ten things you have gratitude for?

Look at the condition of the world, and find your place in it. You'll realize how blessed you are.

Make a habit of counting your blessings every day when you wake up.

Life may be complex and challenging, but there's more than just negativity and hurt. Life is also beauty, love, memories, joy…

The less you focus on what's not going your way and more of what you already have, the more you'll realize how blessed you are. You don't need external validation to give you approval in order to pursue the things you have in heart.

Many people out there have already given up on all hopes for a better life. Sharing your dreams, plans, visions, and goals with them could have a negative influence on your hopes for they will discourage you.

If you're someone who's easily influenced by outside opinions, keep your dreams and goals to yourself.

You don't need people to believe in you.

How do you expect people who don't believe in themselves to believe in you?

You can't bring someone up if they don't wanna get up. You could have the best of intentions but they must want that change themselves.

But the reverse is not true.

A negative person can bring you down because negativity is extremely powerful.

It's like putting a healthy fruit next to a rotten one, the rotten one will contaminate the good one.

Choose your circle wisely.

Think of yourself as a puzzle.

Every time you allow someone to cross your boundaries in order to be liked by them, when you try too hard to please people, when you change yourself to keep others happy and do things that compromise your values, **you give a piece of yourself away.**

And one day, you will give too many pieces away, you will be left feeling empty within and won't know who you are anymore.

You may think it's not a big deal now, but with time, you'll start to realize that you're not doing yourself a favour because people can never be pleased.

Prioritize yourself.

It may seem selfish but sometimes, you just have to do what's best for you, even if it means putting people last.

Being understanding of other people's suffering doesn't mean neglecting your own feelings. You're nobody's punching bag.

You don't have to be nice to people who are rude to you. Sometimes you have to give people a taste of their own medicine so they know how it feels.

People will project their anger on you but understanding their pain doesn't mean allowing them to keep hurting you.

When someone says or does something unintentionally hurtful once, they're being rude. Twice, they're being mean. When it becomes intentional and they keep doing it over even after you tell them to stop, they're being a bully.

Stand up for yourself.

There's nothing normal about being miserable all the time. Being sad is one thing but chronic sadness shouldn't be normalized.

You have to find your peace and happiness. Remember that so many people have been exactly where you are and many of them managed to find their way out, if they could do it, so can you.

Get so sick and tired of feeling the way you're feeling about the things weighing you down. Tired of making excuses to why you can't do and be better.

That's how change will come, by being tired of entertaining the same demons.

You have never truly lived until you have done something for someone who can never repay you.

Touch someone's life.

Do it because you want to leave a positive impact in their lives and give them faith in humanity.

Do it for them, because you want to help them.

But after you do it, don't make it about you by bragging to everyone about what you did.

Find something meaningful that makes you happy. Something you can always return to and enjoy alone in case everyone leaves. Something, not someone.

This will help you live a life that doesn't rely on others to feel fulfilled.

Add people to your life because you want them there, not because you need them. People should only come to your life to add to what's already there.

Have a life of your own outside of all your relationships. Learn to be happy alone. People can make you happy but they should never be your source of happiness.

Don't put the key to your happiness inside someone's pocket.

You have to find meaning within your own life first and then share it with others.

A lot of people can hear you, some can listen to you, but only a few can understand you.

A person who understands you won't put you in a position where you'll constantly have to explain your feelings to them.

Self-care is also choosing to not argue with people who are committed to misunderstanding you.

Your peace sometimes requires you letting some people misjudge you.

To not be understood can be frustrating, but remember that you're not for everyone.

Overthinking will sabotage your reality.

When overthinking, consider asking yourself the following questions:

Are these thoughts mine or are they influenced by my fears, insecurities and unresolved traumas?

Always question the validity of every thought.

What makes them true? Why should you believe them? Is there a better perspective to consider when thinking about a particular situation?

Negative thoughts can only destroy you if you choose to believe they're true.

Your mind is like a garden and your thoughts are the seeds. You can plant flowers or you can grow weeds.

Think of humanity as a body. Some people are the arms, some are the hands, some are the feet, legs, eyes, lips... Each one of us has a part to play to make this body function.

If you're unaware of your purpose, go on a journey of self-discovery. **Get to know yourself in depth**. Because you do have something to bring to this body; you just don't know it.

Being unaware of your purpose doesn't make you useless. It just means you haven't explored yourself yet.

Some people are athletes, musicians, doctors, artists, dancers, comedians, actors, speakers, animal rescuers, etc... You have to find your place.

Have you found your purpose in life yet?

I'm a writer, what about you?

If you find yourself having the same problem with everyone around you, the problem isn't everyone.

Do some shadow work: Uncover parts of yourself that you repress and hide in the darkest part of your soul. Like your traumas or any undesired emotion you don't want to feel.

We create our reality through the thoughts we entertain and the beliefs we hold about these thoughts.

Everyone sees a different truth because everyone is creating what they see. People don't see life as it is, they see life as they are.

If you want to change your reality, start by changing the beliefs you hold about your reality!

Your life is not a screen. You don't need to post things to "prove" to the world that they're happening.

Use social media whichever way you want, just make sure that everything you share is for you, and not because you want to prove yourself or your life to anyone.

Find a way to manage your time online without letting it become toxic to your peace.

Remember, you don't need anyone to validate your life.

The more you seek validation, the emptier you'll feel.

Social media can be a blessing or a curse to your life; it all depends on how you use it and what you use it for.

In everything you do in life, there's always a risk to take.

You'll always risk failure, rejection, getting hurt, being judged, making mistakes…

It's okay to be afraid. Being afraid is normal, but it's what you do when you're afraid that matters.

Fear is temporary but regret is forever.

Do things that scare you.

Try not to make impulsive decisions out of fear, anger or sadness. You will regret it.

Have you ever heard of the 48h rule?

It's allowing your emotions to flow, giving yourself time to cool down by sleeping on your feelings for 48h before deciding.

You must always wait until you feel another emotion to see the situation from a whole different perspective.

Making a decision when you're feeling intense emotions is like going to the store to buy food when you're starving.

You will end up buying things you don't really need.

Don't react, respond!

Don't let people pressure you by making you feel like you're running out of time because you're not where they expect you to be at this stage of your life.

Life doesn't always go as planned. Some people had an advantage over you because their path was less challenging than yours.

While they were building their lives, you were busy trying to survive. It's not the same journey

You will only feel behind in life if you start comparing yourself to other people.

But you have to remember that it's not the same journey. You are not competing with anyone in this life.

What you need to do is focus on yours.

When was the last time you did something that made you really happy? That gave you peace? That made you feel alive?

When was the last time you put yourself first?

Don't get too caught up caring for everyone except yourself. Care for yourself too because if you were to die today, people's lives would go on.

You may as well try to make the best of the life that you have, while you're still here.

Putting yourself first for your own happiness is the best decision you could take in order to live the life you desire. Because a life without memories and happiness is a life gone to waste.

The worst prison is the prison of your mind. Many people are in prison but can't see the bars.

Learn something new everyday. Knowledge is like a map, it will help you navigate through life. It'll give you better insight.

Question everything. Don't blindly follow the crowd. Make good use of your critical thinking skills, you have a brain for a reason. Use it.

People can't control you when you're aware.

Knowledge is power. Awareness is the key.

It doesn't matter how insignificant or irrelevant something you've achieved seems to other people.

If it makes you happy and proud, then it's greater than they think.

The little things you've accomplished so far in your life are important and significant. If doing something made you happy, then nobody has the right to tell you that you're not successful.

People will try to discourage you by comparing you to others to make you feel like you're not doing good enough, they will minimize your accomplishments to make you feel like a failure.

Don't let people who haven't walked in your shoes tell you where you should be in life or how to tie your laces.

They don't know how far you've come.

Once, there was a man who was diagnosed with cancer.

Finding out made him depressed and the symptoms started manifesting all of a sudden in his reality. After a while, the lab called to apologize for misdiagnosing him. He didn't have any major illness. Those results weren't his.

Relieved by the update, his body felt so good all of a sudden and he went back to living his life normally.

Moral of the story:

The mind is powerful. **Once you hold onto a certain belief about yourself and your life, you will start to see it manifest in your reality.**

If you think you won't ever succeed in anything, you will subconsciously keep sabotaging your opportunities.

Just because a pattern is familiar and makes you comfortable, doesn't mean it's healthy. Change your belief system. Think healthy thoughts.

The best way to get your mind off something weighing you down is to redirect your focus on something distracting or uplifting.

Instead of worrying about the things you can't change or control, go read a book, watch a show, do something to keep your mind off overthinking.

Sitting too long in your thoughts will make things worse. Process your emotions, but don't let what you can't control affect your peace.

5 things to quit right now:

1. Overthinking

2. Living in the past

3. Holding onto what no longer serves you

4. Worrying

5. Doubting yourself

Remember that the more you try to control a situation, the more it will end up controlling you.

Desire = attachment = control = suffering

Overthinking is the art of creating problems that don't actually exist.

Take life one day at a time, choose to let go of what no longer serves you best, try to not dwell on your fears, and learn to trust yourself.

There's a fine line between life and death. It's just a breath away. There's no age to die, so never think that you have a lot of time left just because you're young.

None of us knows how much longer we have on earth.

And for this reason, it's important to remind ourselves to live our best lives, to appreciate each day, to love each other, to be humble, more forgiving and understanding towards each other.

Let life flow. Don't stress and worry about the things you can't control.

In the natural flow of life, what will be will be.

When you can't control a situation, trust the flow, let it be. If it's meant to be, it will be. If it doesn't work out, something better will come. Trust it.

Don't hold onto what's too heavy, and don't try to understand life. Surrender and relax.

Have you ever endured so much pain that when something good finally happened, you felt a sudden discomfort?

Happiness and love can look frightening to people who have lived a chaotic life.

I tell you one thing, embrace the good when it comes, don't sabotage it by thinking that it's too good to be true.

You deserve good things in your life too.

Pain isn't supposed to last forever!

There's a time to cry but there's also a time to be happy.

People in your life need to know that their actions have consequences.

Don't diminish yourself for anyone. Don't tolerate toxic behaviour. Be upfront about your boundaries and don't be afraid of losing people or walking away from them.

Let people know that there are certain boundaries they can't cross with you. And if they do, there will be consequences.

Love yourself.

If you ever find yourself on a crossroad not knowing which way to go, don't stress yourself; just do what's best for you.

There are no right or wrong roads, only consequences to our choices. When things don't go as you expect, it doesn't mean it wasn't the right path.

Don't live your life being too wary of making wrong decisions. **It's by failing that you'll gain wisdom**.

It's on you to put in the work needed to get yourself out of whatever situation you're stuck in.

It's up to you to decide whether you want to stay where you are or move forwards. It's on you to make yourself happy.

You will be the one who decides how far you go in this life. It's not on your family, your friends or your partner, but on you.

You are beautiful

You are good enough

You are blessed

You are intelligent

You are capable of achieving great things

You are wonderful

You are loved

The universe, the gods, your ancestors, the angels, or whatever you believe in don't force anything or anyone.

Just because something is happening to you doesn't mean it's your assignment.

Never stay in a toxic situation just because you think there's supposed to be "a blessing behind it." Refuse to become a victim of life. Make better choices!

Always choose peace.

Miserable last year... miserable this year... if you're not careful, you'll be in the exact same spot next year.

The instant you realize that you play a huge part in your happiness and healing, things will start changing for the better.

Life won't magically get better out of nowhere.

It's not your fault that bad things happened to you, but it's your responsibility to find your way out of them.

Do you seriously want to spend the rest of your days being unhappy?

Bring the change you need in your life.

Humility will make you greater than carrying a heart full of pride and ego.

There's a difference between being confident and being full of yourself. Don't ever look down on anyone thinking they're inferior to you. We are nothing but bags of flesh.

Humble yourself or life will do it for you.

ARE YOU AN OLD SOUL?

You have been told you're very mature for your age. You feel like you were born in the wrong decade.

You're highly sensitive and intuitive. You value alone time. You're an introvert.

You feel like a misfit. An outsider. Like you don't belong in this world. You have a hard time finding people to easily connect to.

You struggle with mental illnesses like depression and anxiety.

You're not materialistic; not interested in superficial things. You crave depth in everything. You seek wisdom, truth and knowledge.

You are spiritually inclined and you have spiritual gifts.

You have a lot of compassion and empathy for the world. It makes you attract a lot of broken people.

You rebel against authority. You want to break free from the matrix.

You are creative. You love art. You are art. Art feels like home.

There are things that happen in life that won't ever make sense. No matter how much you'll try to understand, you just won't.

Sometimes, the only closure you need is to accept that life is what it is and things happen because of life, not because of you.

It's not you against life, it's life being life.

Life isn't against you, life just is.

Every time you'll make a decision to become better or to leave something or someone low vibrational behind you, life will test you right away to see if you'll stand.

Your victory will come in the way you handle that test.

You will keep getting tested until you pass.

Life is what it is, and sometimes the unexpected happens at the most unexpected time.

Having a shitty past is not a reason to be a shitty person.

Everyone has been through something traumatic before, but not everyone chose to stay broken.

People who didn't hurt you aren't responsible for your pain. So don't take it out on them.

If someone was in your shoes and came to you for advice, what would you tell them? Sometimes that's the advice you need to give yourself.

You are the best judge of your own situation and every person giving you advice will tell you things from their level of understanding that could leave you even more confused.

There's nothing wrong with seeking answers outside of yourself to validate what you already know deep within. But that's not what life is about.

You and you alone, know exactly what the answers are. Your answers are in your heart, soul, and gut.

The mind is a fickle thing that will always bring in doubt and fear, but you must learn to trust yourself.

The answers you're looking for are right between your ears. Always push for your happiness in life. Push for what your heart is telling you.

This is your journey. Trust yourself.

If you want good things to come to your life, you have to start believing that you deserve them.

How can something good happen to you if you don't even believe that you're worth receiving it in the first place?

You know what I'm saying?

Make sure you're happy in real life too and not just on social media!

Understand timing, destiny and season. You will envy no one.

.

Learn to no longer take things too personally and not let people get the best of your peace whenever they want.

You can achieve this by reminding yourself that you don't have to care and that people's words and actions can only affect you if you allow them to.

If you don't learn to control your emotions and to protect your peace, you're going to cause yourself a lot of suffering.

Does life really have a purpose?

Only if you want it to have one.

The term purpose is more about finding something bigger than yourself to give your experience of existence a greater meaning.

Everyone has their own destiny.

Purpose is about finding your passion, skills, talents and living your life to the best possible use of them.

So challenge your fears, work with your gift. It is yours, use it, share it. You might not end up rich or famous, but you will certainly make yourself happy.

When you're feeling on top in life, when things are going well for you, don't look down on those who are still struggling especially if you once struggled too. Don't forget where you came from by letting pride win you over.

When you're at the bottom, don't compare yourself to those on top. They had their share of struggles too, but they chose to not give up. Do the same.

Life can bless you with good fortune today and take everything away tomorrow.

The same way it can shift you from having absolutely nothing today, to blessing you abundantly tomorrow.

This is why it's important to remain humble when we're on top. And to never lose hope when we're at the bottom.

Give up on limiting beliefs:

False beliefs you've held about yourself for so long that are preventing you from diving into your full potential and improving your life.

Not everything you believe or have been taught is true. Some concepts, beliefs and philosophies should be unlearned.

Reprogram your mind. Unlearn and relearn healthier concepts to improve the quality of your thoughts and help you make better choices for your life.

When a situation makes you feel powerless, one thing you can do to take your power back is to focus on what you can change.

Don't focus on what's not possible, on the power you don't have, on the things you can't control. Flip the coin and focus on the opposites:

What can you do? What can you change? What can you control?

Take life one day at a time. Don't waste too much energy trying to control the things that are out of your control. Just look into your options and ask yourself, what power do I have left?

There's always something you can do, even when it feels like everything is out of control.

And if after exploring all your options, you still can't find a solution, then maybe it's a truth to be accepted rather than a problem to be solved.

You ever wonder why so many people are unhappy in life? Even the ones that seem to have "everything"?

A majority of people have been programmed to believe that to be happy means to have a painless life and to never feel negative emotions.

So they start chasing after "perfection" and get disappointed because after they get what they want, they realize it's not all that there is. Then they want the next thing and it becomes a cycle that leaves them feeling empty every time.

Happiness is both a combination of a mood and a state of mind. It's not a destination of no return.

You can be happy in life and still have sad days. The most important thing is to enjoy the good times when they come and remind yourself that the bad days are only temporary.

Happiness is in the little things of life. You know when you're enjoying your favourite meal and you feel good? That's what happiness looks like.

Some people believe that nothing is a coincidence in life and everything is connected, while some others argue that life is random.

There's no right or wrong way to look at life, there are only ways that work for each one of us. If you hold onto a philosophy that doesn't harm others, it doesn't matter if people disagree with it.

Just because your opinion and perception of things are unpopular doesn't mean you are wrong.

2+2=4 so does 3+1, 5-1 and 4x1

Choosing a path that doesn't meet people's standards and expectations doesn't mean it won't lead you to where you need to be in life.

Don't let anyone influence or control you by putting you in a box. Mental prisons are the worst because they hold limiting beliefs.

Life may look like a labyrinth, but there's more than just one exit. Your experience of life shouldn't be limited to one option. **Explore and find your way out in life**, and remember that you owe nobody an explanation about your choices.

If your life was perfect, if everything was always going as planned and expected, do you really think you'd ever appreciate and value anything?

Without the challenges of life we can't appreciate the good. **Life is supposed to have ups and downs.**

Find a way to navigate throughout your uncertainties without punishing yourself for struggling.

Replace "why is this happening to me" with **"what is this trying to teach me."**

When you're angry, withdraw

When you're inspired, create

When you're sad, purge

When you're tired, rest

When you're hurt, feel

When you're confused, meditate

Hope and Healing

The most powerful thing about time is that it changes.

Just because right now seems to be heading nowhere doesn't mean it will always be this way.

It's a bad season, not a bad life.

There's nothing new under the sun.

Whatever you're going through right now, someone's already been through it too. In case you feel lost or defeated, know you're not alone.

We all deal with pain and struggles differently. Find your way out. The right path will give you clarity and peace.

If you can't run, walk, and if you can't walk, crawl. But whatever you do, don't stay on the same spot. Make some progress.

Slow progress is still progress and it's better than no progress.

When you're on a path towards growth, your mind will always bring you back to the past and remind you of everything you're trying to forget:

"Remember the last time you let someone close and they hurt you? Remember when you tried but failed? Remember?"

This is fear speaking to you. If all you do is listen to that voice, you'll be stuck where you are for the rest of your life.

The only way to bring change in your life is to take a leap of faith!

When you plant a seed, you don't sit there waiting for it to grow. You fertilize the soil and water it from time to time, but you don't sit and wait.

Some things in life will require nothing other than your patience in order to unfold into your reality. Constantly wondering why things aren't happening when you want them, is equivalent to digging out your seed to make sure it's still there and replanting it back. It will only take longer to grow.

The more you obsess over something, the longer it'll take to come. It's like sitting in front of a clock:

When you're in a hurry, time will slow down.

Obsessions cause delays. Life will bring you the things you need, on the right timing. Some things will only come to you when you no longer want them, when you least expect them or when you're not ready for them.

Detach from your expectations and desire to be in control and then let things naturally come to you in due season.

There's a difference between waiting and being patient.

Waiting is stopping everything to have your expectations met. It's focusing on what you want to see happen at the present moment; It's emotionally consuming.

Whereas being patient is having expectations for things to happen without putting your life on hold.

Are you waiting or being patient?

Are you being patient, or just wasting your time?

If you ever feel like you're stuck and that your life isn't making any progress, think about the clock.

Things are always moving forwards even when they feel stagnant. You know why? Because **everyday is a new day.**

The more sleeps, the closer you get to the completion of certain cycles and the beginning of new ones. That's the power of time. Time never moves backwards. You live in time, therefore you move forward in sync with the rhythm of time.

As you're going through this journey of incertitude, keep a journal of gratitude to give yourself hope to hold onto a greater tomorrow.

There's a lot of sadness in the world. But you know what else is out there?

There's nature, there's music, good food and beautiful people.

So go out there and enjoy life. Enjoy the sunshine too.

Life is a gift.

Nobody was born to be unhappy. It's one thing to be sad from time to time but it's another to be completely miserable all the time.

Life is challenging, but it's our responsibility to push through, in order to find serenity in the midst of all the pain. And it all starts with the beliefs we hold about ourselves.

If you go through life believing that you're born to suffer, then that's what you'll get.

You have to change these beliefs; be more optimistic.

There's a time for everything.

A time to cry, a time to laugh.
A time to win, a time to lose.
A time to live, a time to die.

If right now isn't a happy time in your life then maybe it's the time to be sad. But the good news is that the sun will shine again **someday, your broken heart will mend and you will find your smile again.**

Right now, just give it time.

If you enjoyed a normal childhood, you must remember not having to worry about anything, like food or shelter because your parents took care of everything for you, even when they were struggling.

Adopt the same mindset as an adult. When a situation makes you feel out of control, rest it upon whoever's got your back. Could be a belief system, a therapist or just anyone who's supporting you.

You don't have to carry everything on your shoulder. You're only human. It's okay to need help. **We all need each other in this life.**

Nothing just happens in life, everything requires a process. So don't let the obstacles scare you, make you doubt or give up on yourself.

It's like getting into a car. You already know your destination but on your way, you'll face a lot of obstacles like traffic, drunk drivers, and uneasy pedestrians. You may even get into a crash.

The obstacles happen for you, not to you. It's all connected, and with time you'll see the bigger picture.

Focus on your destination!

You go to bed every night planning tomorrow, with no guarantee that you're even going to wake up. That's hope.

The same way you should also have hope that you will find answers and solutions to whatever is weighing you down right now because life is unpredictable.

It takes a second for something to happen to change your whole reality for the better.

You may not know how or when, but you must have hope that this season will end someday, that things won't always stay the way they are, and that you will find your way out.

You did not deserve the hurt you went through. You did not deserve what happened to you.

I'm sorry you had to go through that.

A lot of the people who caused you all that emotional pain are wounded children in adult bodies.

Be extra kind to yourself on days where you're hurting about the things you thought you had healed from.

It's okay to be tired.

Tired of being strong, tired of being positive, tired of hoping, tired of fighting, tired of life, tired of everything.

But just know that things won't always be this way.

It may take days, weeks or even years to get to that one day that will forever change the rest of your life.

Patience is your best option right now, this chapter will pass no matter how long it takes.

I'm so sorry that things didn't work out the way you wanted. It may feel like the end of the world but it's not.

Give up these limiting beliefs that make you think that there's only one person meant for you in this life. And that if you can't be with them, you won't ever find anyone else. It's not true.

You will always have other options.

To every end there's always a new beginning.

Create a folder in your headspace and lock in all the bad and hurtful memories that hold you back from healing yourself. Do it for your own safety and peace.

Every time these memories will try to resurface, shut the folder down. **You don't have to keep revisiting what you're trying to heal from.**

Sometimes the only way to overcome the past is to create new happy memories, and no longer feed off the bad ones.

Don't worry about it.

It's all going to be good. Right now, just take it one step and day at a time, don't put fear upfront, fear is going to stress you out.

You will be fine, you will find a solution, it won't always be this way. Until then, stay hopeful and strong.

Get it off your chest.

Feel every emotion fully as they come: Sadness, anger, confusion, anxiety, all of them.

If you hold onto them, they will become far worse.

Journal your feelings, go to therapy, talk about your pain until the memory of it no longer haunts you.

Every difficult or painful situation holds the possibility of something good even when it feels hopeless.

Sometimes, bad things have to happen for good things to emerge.

Read this out loud:

I'm not going to keep beating myself up for the mistakes I've made.

I needed to make those mistakes to learn from them.

It's okay to mess up. I'm only human.

Why call it a mistake or why even regret it, when at the time you made that decision it was exactly what you wanted?

Unless you were forced to do something out of your will, don't let the unexpected outcome of your choice beat you up.

You did your best but life decided otherwise; **what did that experience teach you?** That's where your focus should be.

Heal your wounds so you won't have to spend the rest of your life bleeding on those trying to love you.

You have to make an effort or else you'll spend the rest of your life stuck on chapter victim.

You can sit there and choose to be miserable about your life or you can decide to do something about the things you can change.

I want you to hold onto life to see what will happen if you don't give up, if you take a leap of faith, if you keep trying.

I want you to see the happy and healed version of yourself; to see the fruit of all your hard work, perseverance and patience.

Hard times do eventually pass, even when everything seems hopeless.

Better days are coming ahead but in order to see them, you need to stay alive.

Trauma doesn't always make people strong. Some people have been so shattered by their circumstances that the wounds left behind permanent emotional scars.

A moment of silence for the people whose trauma gave them mental illnesses. Those who didn't grow thicker skin. Those who became pessimistic and more fragile.

It's okay if you're struggling to heal yourself; but remember, **you are a survivor, at least be proud of yourself for making it this far.**

You can't steer a parked car.

If you want to turn your life around you have to keep moving.

Feeling hopeless is normal but you must find the courage to keep moving by doing something that will give meaning to your life again.

Join an art club, help your community, find a support group, read inspiring stories of people who struggled but who found their way out, meditate, keep a journal.

Have something to look forward to, as you wake up every morning. Even if it's as simple as watering your garden.

As long as you have a reason to want to be here, the feeling of hope will resurface again with time.

Stay strong.

If you're feeling suicidal, please reach out to someone; even a stranger online. Talk to someone about your feelings. Don't keep them to yourself.

Just because you feel hopeless and think people don't care, doesn't mean it's true. Your thoughts aren't always true.

Find the courage to reach out. Start somewhere.

Music is what feelings sound like.
Tears are what feelings taste like.
Allow music to listen to you while you cry.

Heal so you can open yourself to new and better people. Only you can do this.

Don't give people power over your life anymore. They've done enough damage already.

It's time for a new beginning.

Maybe you're not healing because you're trying to find peace around the same people and in the same environment that broke you down.

Sometimes the only way out is to move somewhere new and leave the past behind.

Remove yourself from toxic environments. Stay away from people who hurt you. There's no healing there.

Feeling hopeless? powerless? defeated? tired? lost? confused?

Whatever you are feeling right now, think back on the last time you felt something similar; think about how you climbed out.

This won't spring you out of your state but it should give you some hope that your down state is not permanent.

You are still that person, you're even stronger and wiser now and this time isn't any different.

Find your way out, like you always do.

Sometimes life is beautiful, sometimes it's not.

Sometimes everything is colorful and full of happiness, but sometimes it's grey, void and windy.

The wind doesn't blow in vain and neither does it blow to destroy you. The wind blows to transform you and to bring change into your life.

Life will sometimes have to make you uncomfortable to trigger things to change around you and within you.

The wind will wipe away all the things holding you back from growing into the person you need to become.

Let the wind blow. It will pass after it's done transforming you.

The stigma of being considered an attention seeker when posting about mental health struggles online, is the same reason people bottle their pain in and commit suicide.

"Oh they're just doing it for attention."

But once the person who cried for help dies, the same people will start sharing posts about mental health awareness.

How hypocritical.

Too many people are suffering in silence and can't even speak their feelings out because of judgemental people that lack empathy.

Vulnerability is strength, not weakness. It takes a lot of courage to be vulnerable.

So when someone finds the courage to talk about their pain, let's show them support not judgment.

If you don't succeed in your twenties, you can make it in your thirties and if you don't make it in your thirties, you got your forties, fifties, sixties etc.

Don't limit your life to the timeframe you have set up for yourself. Life doesn't always go as we plan. **Everyone's on a different time frame.** So just because things didn't happen at the time you expected them to, doesn't mean they won't ever happen.

Realistically, it is true that certain things should happen at a certain age, but don't beat yourself down if things don't happen for you at the time you want them to. You can't control life.

Society pressures people to believe that if you don't have your life together by the age of 25, then you're late or a failure. That's not a realistic way to approach life.

Look back at how far you've come and be proud of yourself for everything you've achieved so far, even if you're not where you wish you could be.

Place your hand on your chest. Do you feel that heartbeat? It's called hope.

And as long as you'll be alive, there will always be hope for things to get better.

So don't judge your life based on the chapter you're currently in, **things won't always be this way.**

Reminiscing on the past won't change anything

Unfortunately, life doesn't always give us what we want.

But struggling doesn't mean failing.

Just because you're not where you wish you could be doesn't mean the chapter ends here.

Just because you didn't get the result you wanted doesn't mean the work you put in wasn't worth it.

At least you tried.

Time doesn't heal, it's what you do in time that does.

Nothing is going to change for the better just because you hope it changes. **You must work on that change.**

Take all the time you need to get yourself back on track.

Heal at your own pace but don't stay too long in your pain because time is the only thing you'll never get back.

Words should only be spoken to encourage, to bless, to uplift, to help and to strengthen. Never to destroy, humiliate or sadden others.

A tongue has no bones, but it can break hearts. Be careful what you tell people.

People are out there still trying to heal from words that were spoken to them in their childhood.

Words are extremely powerful.

You can tell someone something today, and it's gonna take them months or even years to heal from.

There's never a reason to be mean to people. If we can't say anything nice, it's best to say nothing at all.

Telling a person who has a mental illness, to just be happy, is not gonna make them feel better.

Mental illnesses are not choices or easy to climb out of. People are trapped in their minds because of their traumas and it's not voluntary.

Assist a loved one struggling by just being there for them, be a listener. **People don't always need advice but they definitely need love.**

When you hit rock bottom and feel like it's the end, that's when life can mysteriously take a U-turn and throw you out in the light.

Not all stories have happy endings, but you'll never know how yours will end unless you hold onto life to see what will happen if you don't give up.

So when you're going through a rough time, pause and tell yourself the following:

I want to see what will happen if I don't give up on myself and on my life. I want to see the fruits of my hard work, my patience, my perseverance, and the reward for all my tears and hustle.

Nothing lasts forever. There will come a time where you will get a break from suffering. It might take months or years but no condition is permanent because change is consistent.

To all the people making the world a better place with your love and kindness.

Thank you.

It's people like you that give me faith in humanity.

Our planet needs a lot of love and healing.

Sending out love and positive energy to all who are fighting silent battles. To those of you who are feeling stuck in loops; hurts and situations that are out of your control.

To people struggling to find healing, peace and clarity because everything is so deeply painful and complicated.

To those who are desperate for a change but who just don't know how to get out of these turmoils.

May grace find your way so that your life can have meaning again. It won't rain forever.

Look for something positive in each day, even if that means having to look a little harder some days.

I hope that you get to a point in your life where you realize that the little things are actually the big things. That every moment, experience and feeling, counts.

Live, don't just exist. Be happy, express your truth. Don't hold grudges. Don't live in regrets. Don't hide behind a facade. Be authentic, kind, loving, giving, humble.

Because at the end of your life, **what will matter the most is the kind of life you created for yourself.** So make the best of everything while you're still here.

BE NNSPIRED

Facebook: NavecQuotes
Youtube: NavecQuotes
Instagram: Quotesby.navec
Email: navecquotes@gmail.com

About the author

Naomi Navec, author of *Mystery School*, is an inspirational and motivational writer who began writing at the age of ten. She has written about different genres of literature and now as an adult, she chose to focus on mental health. Her goal is to give people hope.

"I have been in a place in my life where I felt so hopeless, but words saved me. I write to give people hope so they feel less alone and more understood. This journey called life is challenging and it takes a strong mind to make it through. Words are powerful, they make a difference."

Navec founded Born To Nnspire in 2015; she believes that her life purpose is to inspire people with her words.

BORN TO NNSPIRE

Printed in Great Britain
by Amazon